THE SKY IS HOME

THE SKY IS HOME

The Story of
Embry-Riddle Aeronautical
University
1926-1986

by
John McCollister
and
Diann Ramsden

jD Jonathan David Publishers, Inc.
Middle Village, New York 11379

THE SKY IS HOME
Copyright © 1986
by
Embry-Riddle Aeronautical University

No part of this book may be reproduced in any manner or form
without the prior writtern consent of the publishers. Address all
inquiries to:

Jonathan David Publishers, Inc.
68-22 Eliot Avenue
Middle Village, New York 11379
10 9 8 7 6 5 4 3 2 1

Library of Congress Cataloging in Publication Data

McCollister, John.
  The sky is home.

  Includes index.
  1. Embry-Riddle Aeronautical University—History.
I. Ramsden, Diann. II. Title.
TL560.2.E49M38   1986   629.13'007'1175919   86-16661
ISBN 0-8246-0321-4

Printed in the United States of America

"For most people, the sky is the limit; for those who love aviation, the sky is home." —Jack R. Hunt

★ . . . . ★ . . ★ . . . . . . ★ . . . . . ★ . . ★★ . . ★ . . . . ★

Table of Contents

Acknowledgments

The family of Embry-Riddle Aeronautical University applauds the conscientious efforts of all those who compiled, wrote, and edited the written and oral testimonies about the University's foundation and development.

Ms. Diann Ramsden gathered the bulk of the material from the Embry-Riddle archives and through visits to the Cincinnati Historical Society, the newspaper department of the Hamilton County (Ohio) Library, and Lunken Airport.

Dr. John McCollister wrote the narrative based upon this research as well as additional oral testimony.

Special thanks must be given to Mr. James H Straubel, a member of Embry-Riddle's Board of Trustees, who supplied some of the color of the era when Mr. Embry and Mr. Riddle "hand-propped" their first airplane in 1926. Also, we recognize the efforts of Dr. Janet Preston of the Prescott, Arizona Campus for her input.

Among those who edited and reviewed this text were: Mr. Eric Doten, Mr. John Fidel, Mr. W. James Harman, Ms. Lynne Hunt, Mr. Virk Legate, Mr. Ronald Marlar, Dr. Roger Osterholm, Lt. Gen. Kenneth Tallman, Mrs. Dianne Thompson, and, of course, Mr. Paul Riddle.

Finally, those who worked on this project thank their families for their support during the creation of this long-awaited story of Embry-Riddle.

★★★★★ . . ★★ . . . . ★ . . . . ★ . . . . . . ★ . . . . . .

Introduction

This is the story of a university.

The word "story" is purposely used in lieu of the common designation "history." An institution of higher education rarely has a history in the strict sense of the word. Instead, as bestselling author Robert Serling (an honorary alumnus of Embry-Riddle) suggests, the record of its foundation and growth more closely resembles a biography. A private school, perhaps more than any other entity, resembles a human personality—usually because each campus mirrors the character of the individuals who created, nurtured, and guided it.

While many institutions never got beyond the planning stage, those that were able to begin and survive did so amid fierce competition from state schools, internal power struggles, and daring decisions. In spite of all the barriers thrown up to check their advance, the successful private colleges and universities share two legacies: bold leaders and priceless loyalty to the school.

11

In 1701, for instance, 10 Connecticut clergymen met in the village of Branford and donated books to found a college. In addition, the clergymen outlined the guiding principles that still serve as the foundation for what is known today as Yale University.

Likewise, in 1875, the dynamic and forceful Mormon leader Brigham Young shaped a university that bears his name so that students could study the dogma of their faith without fear of persecution.

Embry-Riddle Aeronautical University shares much of this same spirit, but with a few unique twists.

Were Embry-Riddle to embody the distinct personalities of all the leading characters in its development, it would create a psychologist's nightmare. The leaders who shaped its history form a collage of contrasts. Begun by two men— one whose main love was flying, the other whose primary philosophy was to enjoy life to the hilt—Embry-Riddle's standardbearers included the nation's first woman president of a flying school, a man who was forced to resign after serving less than six months, a former U.S. Navy commander who won the Harmon International Trophy, yet had no prior experience as a school administrator, and a three-star general who once headed the U.S. Air Force Academy.

The saga of Embry-Riddle is peppered with sharp peaks and valleys. The recorded memories portray a roller-coaster ride of prosperity and demise. The once-prosperous flying school literally closed its doors for nine years, only to be reborn when America was on the brink of war.

After a decade marked with relocations and name changes, Embry-Riddle's administration dared to make some bold decisions. As a result, enrollments steadily increased, course offerings were expanded, and a university was born.

Those who guided Embry-Riddle possessed the robust spirit of individualism so common within the aviation community. Yet, somehow, those egos were suppressed—often at the urging of a more powerful ego—and blended into a unified effort to mold the University into the world's leader in aviation higher education.

This, then, is the story of Embry-Riddle and of the men and women dedicated to the proposition that students must be prepared to face every challenge aviation has to offer—from landing a single-engine biplane on a tiny grass strip in Cincinnati, to launching a space shuttle from the pad at the Kennedy Space Center.

1

I Wanted to Fly

J. Paul Riddle in the cockpit of an early biplane. Riddle currently resides in Coral Gables, Florida, and is Founder Trustee of Embry-Riddle Aeronautical University. He frequently visits the campuses at Daytona Beach, Florida, and Prescott, Arizona.

"The Air Corps tried to send me to balloon school. But I didn't want to learn anything about balloons. I wanted to fly airplanes." —J. Paul Riddle, 1920

John Paul Riddle

He was only 18 years old, but he knew what he wanted out of life. One thing he knew he *didn't* want was a full-time military career. In fact, he initially declined the coveted appointments to both the U.S. Naval Academy and to West Point, although he finally accepted an appointment to Annapolis.

His name was John Paul Riddle. The year was 1920—only 17 years after the Wright Brothers flew their "Flyer" on its initial voyage of 12 seconds, covering all of 120 feet.

It was the beginning of a decade described by Isabel Laighton as "The Aspirin Age." The Twenties was an era when the Charleston and Eliot Ness were in vogue. People sang "Yankee Doodle Dandy." The stock market was going up; women's skirts were going down. Flappers, gangsters, and bathtub gin were paraded across the nation to the beat of a brash new sound of music called "jazz."

Americans in the "Roaring Twenties" celebrated life with gusto. After all, they had just fought and won the "war to end all wars."

17

Aviation was still in the kindergarten of development. Aerial antics were introduced to the general public at county fairs by former Army pilots who barnstormed their way from town to town in war-surplus planes purchased for 300 dollars.

The air shows of these "flying gypsies" were staged to lure the more daring spectators on "joyrides" at 10 dollars for one trip "around the patch."

Although unorganized and expensive, aviation's mystique lured those who dared to rise above the earth.

John Paul Riddle was one of those people.

"I tried to join the Air Corps as a cadet as a way of learning to fly," said the six-foot, 140-pound native of Pikeville, Kentucky, "but, because of budget restrictions, they could not send me to flying school. They could send me to balloon school. However, I didn't want to learn anything about balloons. I wanted to fly airplanes."

Finally, the Air Corps agreed to send Riddle to its Air Service Mechanics School at Kelly Three Field in San Antonio, Texas.

"I spent a solid year learning how to build, repair, and maintain airplanes, engines, and accessories," he confessed, "and it was the best thing that ever happened to me. When I started taking planes into the air, I knew what made them tick. If something went wrong, I knew what it was, and I could fix it."

He completed mechanics school in 1921 and received his appointment as a cadet. He moved with the mechanics school from San Antonio to Chanute Field in Rantoul, Illinois, then to Carlstrom Field in Arcadia, Florida for flight training.

He and his fellow cadets were limited to only five flying hours a month following their primary training, due to budget restrictions. Other cadets, however, seemed to be interested not so much in flying, but in what Sarasota, Ft. Myers, and other nearby Florida cities had to offer. They willingly relinquished their unused flying hours to Riddle who, as a result, accumulated more flying time than any other cadet on the field.

Soon he transferred to Post Field at Fort Sill, Lawton, Oklahoma, where he would learn, firsthand, about the value of sound construction. The Air Service there was rebuilding de Havilland DH-4s with Liberty engines. They were attached to an airframe unceremoniously dubbed "The Flying Coffin" because it could not withstand the pressures of aerobatics.

"On my first day there, my instructor took me up in one of those de Havillands," Riddle explains. "He takes me up about five thousand feet and says to me: 'Spin me down to thirty-five hundred.'"

"What?" I asked.

"Go on. Spin it," he said.

"Really spin it?"

"Yes," he demanded.

"So, I did. Nothing happened. I pulled it out at thirty-five hundred feet. It was smooth as silk."

"See? They make 'em a lot stronger and safer now."

"That," said Riddle, "showed me the importance of solid engineering."

Riddle received advanced training as an observation pilot when his entire observation unit was moved to Kelly Field, Texas. Both Riddle and one of his classmates, George McGinley—a former All American from Nebraska—wanted to share the adventure with others. Together they were able to muster $250 and purchase a used Jenny aircraft.

On weekends, they took off from Kelly Field to parts unknown, barnstorming around the state, giving rides to passengers for five or six dollars. "Sometimes pretty girls flew for free," says Riddle.

"I kept the plane hangared at Kelly Field," remembers Riddle. "My commanding officer was afraid that I might get hurt, so he ordered his operations officer to see that the plane was in number one condition at all times. Heck, they did all the work taking care of it. I had all the fun flying it."

Not only were his barnstorming trips profitable, but, after his stint with the military, Riddle was also earning a solid reputation as a pilot and an instructor.

THE SKY IS HOME

Lewis Stone, a former neighbor who had more money than experience, owned two airplanes and was instructing about 10 students. His fees were quite high—$300 for 10 hours of flying. At the same time, he was not a successful teacher.

"I'm having problems," he confessed to Riddle. "I get up with these students, and the plane starts to go over, and I can't properly control it."

"How much time have you had?" asked Riddle.

"Well . . . I went down to Huntington, West Virginia and bought this airplane. They gave me one solo flight, then sent me home. I guess I have . . . ah . . . eight and a half hours. Three of them have been instructing."

"I couldn't believe it," Riddle recalls. "No wonder so many kids were killed in those days."

Over the next few months, Riddle instructed both Stone and his students, stressing the importance of safety—a dimension of aviation that he maintained could not be emphasized too much. Gangsters were labeled "public enemies" by law enforcement officials; to John Riddle Public Enemy Number One was "pilot error," a killer which he fought like a G-man policing the still-dangerous sport of aviation.

Although safety was a prevailing concern, Riddle was not above employing a flair for the dramatic. Once when a passenger hired him to fly to Cincinnati, Riddle chose to land on a polo field which was close to the passenger's destination. Unfortunately, a game was in progress that Sunday afternoon. Riddle continued to circle the field, until both sides called a time-out between chukkers. Riddle promptly set the plane down on the field in front of some mildly disturbed spectators who thought the game might have to be postponed. Riddle maneuvered the plane to the sidelines and, while waiting for his passenger to return, demonstrated his uncanny ability to turn a problem into a profit.

Instead of arguing with the people, he convinced some of them to experience the thrill of flight . . . for a fee, of course.

Those who accepted his invitation became instant evangelists for flight. Many lost themselves in bold gestures and superlatives while describing to their friends and neighbors the magnificent view of life from a new perspective. Consequently, others wanted to share the thrill. Riddle enrolled enough students that afternoon to justify operating a small passenger-carrying service in Cincinnati. When business lagged, he returned to Pikeville and barnstorming, giving exhibition flights for county fairs and other celebrations.

Riddle predicted that Cincinnati was going to be a forerunner in aviation. In August 1923 he bought a Hisso Standard plane and set up a flying business at Besuden Field near Carthage. The business boomed until cold weather intervened.

They followed the sun to Ashland, Kentucky for more barnstorming, then continued on to more than a dozen states.

"When business was dull, we cut the price," admits Riddle. "When it was good, we raised it as high as we could go. In the eyes of these people, the 'Red Baron' had nothing on us. We were genuine heros. We pocketed the money and basked in glory. That was my introduction to aviation management."

But financial income generated from barnstorming was, at best, sporadic. Riddle was eventually lured away by what appeared to be a more secure position with Griswold Air Service in Erie, Pennsylvania. After only a few months, however, he returned to Cincinnati to meet with a former student who would have a profound effect on his life and career.

The former student was T. Higbee Embry, a rather wealthy free spirit who suggested that the two of them become the distributors for Waco Aircraft in Ohio, Indiana, and Kentucky. With the signing of an agreement in December 1925, the Embry-Riddle Company was formed.

Talton Higbee Embry

T. Higbee Embry, a native of Cincinnati, first met Riddle in 1923. Riddle was then operating a small flying business at Besuden Field, which included selling rides to anyone who came by. One of the first to approach Riddle was Mr. Embry.

"How much for a ride?" asked Embry.

T. Higbee Embry, co-founder of the Embry-Riddle Company, left the enterprise in 1930 and moved to California, where he died in 1946. Embry and Riddle remained close friends through their pioneering partnership and afterward.

"How much do you have with you?" responded Riddle.

"Twenty dollars," he said.

"That's exactly the price. Hop in," said Riddle.

The rather expensive airfare notwithstanding, Embry did not complain. Indeed, he was hooked. Within a few days, he bought his own airplane—a Waco 9 (the first one produced by Advance Aircraft Company)—and hired Riddle for flying lessons.

Embry was an excellent student. He soloed in only seven hours.

Both Riddle and Embry developed a strong relationship during these days of instruction that grew beyond the teacher-student roles to a mutual respect for each other. Embry became convinced that his enthusiasm for life, combined with Riddle's flying expertise, would be the ideal raw materials for a profitable business in aviation. Riddle agreed.

On December 17, 1925—the 22nd anniversary of the Wright Brothers' first flight—Embry handed Riddle the agreement and a pen with which to sign. Everything was now in place for the actual start of business in 1926.

The Embry-Riddle Company

The Embry-Riddle Company began with two Jenny airplanes and a dream.

Its first venture was selling Waco Aircraft. The contract with the manufacturer guaranteed that a total of 12 airplanes would be delivered at one-month intervals. Embry and Riddle agreed to sell them as quickly as possible and to notify the manufacturer when the order needed to be increased.

Waco fulfilled its promise. Five planes were delivered over the next five months, right on schedule. Unfortunately, Embry-Riddle could find no buyers.

"I felt so sorry for myself and Riddle," said Embry. "My heart sank when I saw those five Wacos sitting silently in the hangar just staring at us."

Embry dug into his savings and bought one himself; his mother, now an officer of the Company, bought another.

Embry-Riddle Company Office in Cincinnati, Ohio. The headquarters of the company were here at the Lunken Airport from 1926 to 1930, when the airport and the company were considered "synonymous."

The next few weeks were more rewarding. Both Embry and Riddle became more aggressive, combed the countryside, and located four buyers. Before the year ended, they sold a grand total of 14 aircraft.

"We knew we could do it, although there were moments at the beginning when we had it plenty rough," Embry confessed. "Others may have thrown in the towel, but that thought never crossed our minds. We were determined to make it. People often asked me if there was money in aviation. I told them, 'You're damn right. I ought to know. I put it there.'"

With the sales came both profits and other contracts. The Company expanded its operation at Lunken Airport in Cincinnati. The *Cincinnati Post* applauded the growth:

> Regular commercial aviation service for Cincinnati is available as a result of an agreement between Army officials and controllers of the Embry-Riddle Company, airplane operators, which provides for joint occupancy of Lunken Airport.

The Lunken Airport was a genuine "home" to Riddle. "This was the same polo field in which I landed on my first flight to Cincinnati three years earlier," he said.

Other Ventures

Even before expanding at Lunken airport, the Company had inaugurated a new service—a flying school. A prominent businessman named John Pattison was the first student to solo. He was followed by scores of men and women who dared to leave the bonds of earth for a "trip through the heavens," as some of the more poetic enthusiasts phrased it.

Other services soon followed. "One of our first 'odd jobs' was to drop circulars for a Covington, Kentucky store. They paid us two-hundred fifty dollars just for doing that," said Embry. "It was extremely windy that day. I remember when we dumped the circulars, they flew for miles. I wonder how many of them actually landed in Covington."

THE SKY IS HOME

When Embry and Riddle chose to participate in the famous "Ford Reliability Tours"—a promotion sponsored by Edsel Ford to demonstrate the practicability of cities having airports for this fast-growing method of transportation—they made a unique impression. Riddle not only flew the Waco owned by Mrs. Susan Embry (Higbee's mother), but also took her along as a passenger. She was the only woman on tour that year.

This was no publicity stunt. Riddle openly encouraged women to share in the thrill of flight.

"Women have more nerve than men when it comes to flying," claimed Riddle. "They are always more eager to go aloft, seem to enjoy it more than men, and invariably want to go up again and again. Maybe it's because women are naturally nearer to angels than are men."

The Company received national recognition when one of the pilots loaded film taken of the 1928 Kentucky Derby in Louisville and flew it to Ohio in time to load it aboard the train for New York for use by the International News Service the next day.

Neither Embry nor Riddle shunned publicity. They knew that a well-placed story could generate more business. On one occasion they asked the students of the University of Cincinnati to select a classmate whom Riddle's instructors would teach to solo in only one day.

"We did it just to show that learning to fly was not as difficult as many came to believe," said Riddle.

The student, Frank Sheldon, arrived at the airport at precisely 9:30 the next Saturday morning. Five and a half hours later, after an incredible number of 74 landings, young Sheldon took the plane around the field and brought it back with a perfect "three point landing."

Employees of the Company formed a "speakers' bureau" and appeared on a weekly radio show on Station WLW to answer questions about aviation.

While the company's pioneers never overlooked an opportunity for a good story, they never compromised on the importance of safety. Newspaper reporters of the day regularly used words such as "cautious" and "extremely careful" when describing the Embry-Riddle operation. One reporter wrote about Paul Riddle: "If he lives to be 120 years old, he will undoubtedly retain all of his fingers and toes because of his steadfast refusal to take unnecessary hazards."

The constant awareness of safety was a theme trumpeted by Embry, Riddle, and every member of the Company team. Their persistence did not go unrewarded. The Company was commended in 1927 for flying 330,000 miles without a personal injury.

In December of that year, Contract Airmail Route 24, from Cincinnati, via Indianapolis, to Chicago, was awarded to Embry-Riddle. Several factors contributed to this selection as reported in Cincinnati's *Commercial Tribune*:

> The personnel and character of all firms bidding on air mail are vital considerations in the awarding of contracts. These facts were factors in the selection of the Cincinnati firm. Although the youngest, being but two and a half years old, it has already gained a name for itself throughout the industry by its aggressiveness, the quality of its flying school, and the high tone of operation maintained at Lunken Airport.

The mail service began that year on December 17—the date made famous in 1903 by the Wright Brothers' first airplane flight—and was ushered in with the red carpet treatment by the city. The *Commercial Tribune* carried a two-page spread; a motor parade escorted the mail truck to the airport; federal authorities, city officials, merchants, and professional men made certain they had front row seats. At 3:30 p.m., pilot Stanley "Jiggs" Huffman took off in the Waco painted a bright orange and silver (the adopted colors of the Embry-Riddle fleet) with a cargo of 7,200 letters and packages, while the onlookers cheered and applauded.

Cincinnati thus became one of the few cities to have

Flight instructors and air mail pilots. A sample company advertisement from the March 1929 issue of the house organ *Sky Traffic* pictures some of the early pilots.

direct mail service. The West Coast and the South were now three days closer.

Not only did Embry-Riddle win in competitive bidding, its performance record was so high that it was one of only two companies (the other was Boeing Air Transport) authorized by the Government to fly passengers as well.

Robert Serling, in his book *Eagle, the Story of American Airlines,* reports that passengers who flew with the mail were also pioneers of a sort. Prior to take-off, they were given a small box of provisions that might be deemed the first in-flight service. Each box contained an apple, a small sandwich, chewing gum, some cotton for the ears, and two small ammonia capsules—the standard treatment for airsickness.

Passengers did not enjoy the luxury of choice between first-class and coach accommodations. Instead, each one was required to sit on mailbags in the open cockpit in front of the pilot.

For some of the passengers, this was their introduction to flight. It was not for the fainthearted. Flying was still regarded by most as a dare-devil stunt. Those brave enough to climb aboard what many considered to be little more than "fabric-covered deathtraps" and fly cross-country often boasted of their prowess for months thereafter.

Charles Planck, Embry-Riddle's first public relations officer, suggested a psychological aid for the more timid. He asked the pilots to carry two boxes of dirt on the floor of the front cockpit into which passengers could rub their feet and feel the crunch of earth. It was a gimmick, perhaps, but it had astounding results.

Pilots who flew these routes for Embry-Riddle would rather fly than eat. They were paid at the rate of only 10 cents a flying mile, with no base pay, and no differential for night flying. The pilots did not object, however, since the routes were over level ground, an important safety consideration.

Embry-Riddle, like every other mail carrier, was compelled to count every nickel. Air mail did not provide the carriers with an avalanche of profits. The Government paid a maximum of three dollars for every pound of mail flown. When there wasn't enough mail to cover the cost of gasoline for the trip, some of the more inventive carrier pilots stuffed mail sacks with wet blotters, wrapped bricks, even bags of dirt—all with mailing labels, of course.

Air mail pilots flying cross-country often relied upon the crudest instruments—a compass, an altimeter, a watch, and the seat of their pants.

Their most often-used landmark was a highway, a telephone line, or a railroad track (dubbed an "iron compass"). When pilots were "on the rails," and a tunnel suddenly popped up out of nowhere, it could spell disaster. With no radio beam to guide them and no accurate way to measure ground speed, pilots who flew above the overcast could use only dead reckoning to know where they were or when to descend.

A rather creative Army pilot, Jimmy Doolittle, was working on a more reliable solution to the problem. He was engaged at McCook Field in the center of Dayton in the experiments that resulted in his famous totally "blind flight" one year later at Roosevelt Field, New York. Doolittle and his staff passed on these findings to J. Paul Riddle who, in turn, shared them with his students. The School used this new information to modify one of its training planes. Thus, Embry-Riddle became one of the first institutions to offer instrument flight instruction.

In just two years, Embry-Riddle had grown from a little-known airplane distributor to a multi-dimensional aviation enterprise receiving national attention.

One cannot help but wonder if T. Higbee Embry even dared to dream about this much success on that memorable afternoon in 1926 when his heart sank at the sight of those five unsold aircraft gathering dust in the hangar.

★★★★★★★★★★★★★★★★★★★★★★★★

2

From School to Airline

★★★★★★★★★★★★★★★★★★★★★★★★

An Embry-Riddle Waco biplane in 1927. Pictured standing behind one Waco biplane of the "E-R Express" are (from left to right) Paul Riddle, Richard Blythe, T.H. Embry, Charlie Myers, John Woods, and Harry Sherwin.

"We start into a new year which we know will be crammed full of history in aviation—packed with events and progress that we can't even imagine."

—T. Higbee Embry, 1929

A Growing Reputation

Mr. Embry's fears had long since given way to smiles. By 1928, the Embry-Riddle Company owned six planes for the flying school, eleven for the air mail service, and two for cross-country flying. Fifty-four people, including 30 pilots, were on its payroll. In addition, the Company was now a sales agent not only for Waco but also Monocoupe and Fairchild aircraft.

Since its organization, it had sold 149 airplanes, which presented a new, rather pleasant problem—the Company had to find ways to get faster deliveries from the factories to keep pace with the orders.

The air mail business increased a whopping 112 percent. The Embry-Riddle air mail line was the only one in the country to show a 100-percent increase in poundage, according to one report. One of the reasons for this phenomenal growth was that the Company maintained its schedule 94 percent of the time.

"That was a hell of a lot better than even the slower trains," said Embry.

Through all of this increase and solid record of punctuality, the Company never forgot the importance of air safety. From 1927 to 1929, more than 22,000 passengers flew under the colors of the Embry-Riddle Company with not one being injured.

Punctuality and safety were noble qualities, indeed. but if aviation were to become attractive to the public, innovative appeals had to be used. and Paul Riddle was a master at creating new ideas that caught the public's imagination.

In December 1929, Riddle offered flying lessons as Christmas gifts. These certificates were sold not at airports, but from the counters of department stores, cigar stores, and gift shops.

"If aviation expected to thrive," he said, "we had to reach out to where the people were."

The plan worked. Parents bought rides for their children. Pilots bought certificates for reluctant neighbors who swore: "Someday, I'm gonna' go up in one of those planes."

Air shows and air races of this era brought crowds of more than 50,000 people to an airport on Sunday afternoons. Often the crowd at Lunken Field in Cincinnati surpassed those at any sporting event in the nation that day—including those who watched Babe Ruth and the mighty Yankees in New York.

Another means of reaching out to the general public was through the Air Information Bureau begun by the Company in 1928. Some historians claim that this was the world's first travel agency. The Bureau, located at the Gibson Hotel in Cincinnati, offered information on every air mail and passenger line in the world that operated on a given day. Through the Bureau, customers could find the best routes, the rates, and connecting bus or train schedules.

"We took care of all the details," said Riddle. "All the people had to do was bring their suitcases and follow our directions. It was as simple as that."

Simple, perhaps, but no one had ever thought of it before.

The idea caught on. Later that year, Embry-Riddle, in cooperation with other air mail carriers, opened a similar operation, called "The Consolidated Airline Tickets Office," at the Palmer House in Chicago.

Safety

Due, in part, to the success of the Embry-Riddle Company, other flight schools were opened throughout America. Unfortunately, some seemed more concerned about turning a fast profit instead of offering quality instruction with safety.

One outspoken advocate for safety was Lt. Barrett Studley of the U.S. Navy who wrote: "The operation of these schools is of vital concern, not only to the student, but to everyone interested in aviation." The lieutenant explained: "For every student who, half-trained and ill-prepared, wrecks his plane on an early solo flight, ten other prospective airplane buyers are discouraged."

The airplane manufacturers listened to Lt. Studley's warning with more than just passing interest. The number of future sales would be in direct proportion to well-trained new pilots.

Lt. Studley, in other articles and speeches delivered throughout the country, took exception to the poor quality of instruction offered at many schools. "A flight instructor," he said, "must be able to analyze mistakes, determine the causes, and explain them to the student so that he will understand. The responsibility of the flight schools is to share effective methods to not only teach flying, but also to correct or avoid common mistakes."

"Not all men can fly safely," he continued. "A flight school cannot escape the responsibility of separating those who can from those who cannot. It takes ten hours of dual flight to determine if someone has a satisfactory aptitude for this unforgiving concept called 'flying.'"

In contrast to the schools that were the targets of the

lieutenant's wrath, Embry-Riddle enjoyed a solid reputation for teaching flying skills with safety.

Mr. Embry explained: "There are two types of commercial aviation—the 'aviation enterprise' and the 'aviation racket.' The 'aviation racket' pictures a well-dressed pilot with limited knowledge, flying a brightly-painted airplane with loose fabric and a noisy engine. This 'racket' is one real obstacle to the progress of aviation. Embry-Riddle will have no part of an 'aviation racket.' "

The editor of *Air Transportation* agreed when he wrote in 1928: "Every once in a while, someone comes along and develops an air school to the point where the school means a lot more than the school of earlier days. Embry-Riddle is to be congratulated for the high standards on which they conduct their school."

Another writer reported: "The Embry-Riddle Flying School is not only one of the best in the country, but is one of the best equipped."

The high standards were embodied in the philosophy of the School as spelled-out in its first official catalog in 1928:

> We believe that the student should learn in a school employing only licensed pilots and modern licensed planes.
>
> It should have financial and moral standing and stability in back of every statement or promise. It should have and merit the good will and respect of the entire industry.
>
> It should provide a thorough ground school training, with competent instructors, so that there will be an adequate background of the theory of flight to form the basis of a student's advancement in the profession of flying or to enhance his skill at the controls in flying for sport or pleasure.
>
> It should adhere strictly to the rules of the U.S. Dept. of Commerce, Aeronautics Branch, governing flying schools, both in spirit as well as technically.
>
> It should be conscientious, its diplomas presented for

Two Monocoupes and a biplane. Three of the Embry-Riddle fleet in the late 1920s.

evidence of skill and knowledge attained only, and not for the mere cost of tuition.

The School's first formal commencement exercises conducted on the flight line, July 29, 1928, featured Stanley "Jiggs" Huffman, Operations Officer of the School, who delivered the commencement address. He, too, took this opportunity to stress the importance of flight safety: "Learn your limitations," he warned the students. "Know when to quit. People may say about you, 'That so-in-so is a mediocre pilot.' They might say, 'You are yellow.' Don't worry. You would rather hear them say these things than to hear them say, 'He WAS a good pilot.' "

Flying as a Profession

Embry-Riddle had the unique position of contributing to the development of aviation as an employer and as a trainer of pilots. The Company was constantly on the lookout for pilots for its rapidly growing air passenger, air mail, and air express services, not to mention airplane sales.

As an employer, it recognized the responsibility in training students to meet its own demands, plus those of the industry.

Charles Planck wrote in a 1929 issue of *Aviation* Magazine: "The [Embry-Riddle] Company has realized the imperative needs of pilots, and is constantly on the lookout among its students for likely material for its own pilot force."

"We were at the point where we could be more selective than others," admitted Riddle. "We chose to make professionals out of those who had the right material and attitude."

One instructor put it more bluntly: "If they are the right type, we urge them on; if not, we drop them, because there are a lot more waiting."

And more were waiting. From October 1928 through January 1929, the School averaged 100 letters of application each week.

Embry-Riddle School of Aviation

(APPROVED BY THE U. S. DEPT. OF COMMERCE)

LUNKEN AIRPORT, CINCINNATI, OHIO

This Certifies that LIONEL STEPHAN having successfully completed the Prescribed Course of Flying and Ground School, is awarded this

Given at LUNKEN AIRPORT this 13 day of MARCH 1928

_____ Instructor

S.C. Huffman Flying Instructor

_____ Chief Instructor

_____ President

_____ Treas.

One of the early graduation certificates from the Embry-Riddle School of Aviation.

Riddle's standards were known to be high; they were now even more rigid.

"It takes two years to become a professional pilot," he insisted.

Those two years were packed with instruction and safety awareness. The primary course included 10 hours of dual instruction, one hour of solo time, and 30 hours of ground school. Students in the advanced course flew another 50 hours of solo with frequent check rides and corrective counsel. Following those 50 hours, the candidate had to pass a written examination. If successful, he received a "limited commercial pilot's license." Only after adding another 200 hours of flying time to his log book could he earn a transport pilot license.

The Company made a distinction between teaching someone to fly and training someone to be a pilot. Instructors of the School maintained that anyone can "fly" after having a primary course and one hour of solo, but he is not yet a "pilot." Furthermore, 50 hours of solo flying and ground courses do not make fliers worth very much to industry. To be a pilot, claimed the School's instructors, the individual needs the primary and advanced courses, along with the ground courses and flying experience in many types of aircraft. He needs experience in airport and airline management, as well as hangar and maintenance work. "This way," said "Jiggs" Huffman, "the graduates of Embry-Riddle will be safe fliers and assets to the industry."

Mr. Riddle had another way of identifying the promising student. "I watched how a person treated the aircraft when he taxied to the ramp. If he was a 'hot dog,' I didn't want him. And I told him so, as soon as he climbed out of the plane."

Other schools apparently did not share Mr. Riddle's concerns. The lack of uniform quality of flying schools drew the ire of national figures such as Sen. Hiram Bingham of Connecticut, who in 1928 sponsored an amendment to the Air Commerce Act that would require an annual examination and rating of civilian flying schools. He wrote: "The Aeronautics Branch of the Department of Commerce daily is flooded with requests from people who ask: 'where can I obtain a good, reliable course in flying?' Owing to the lack of standardization, stabilization, or rating of the flying schools in existence today, this vitally important information cannot be given."

Others joined in urging the adoption of this amendment. The *Air Commerce Bulletin*, an official D.O.C. publication, reported in 1929:

> The greatest number of accident causes are chargeable to personnel, and the greatest contributing factor in this category is poor technique on the part of the pilot. This, of course, reflects upon the flyer's original training and leads to the inevitable conclusion that still higher standards in flying schools are necessary.

The amendment was passed with ease. The terms of the amendment were to be administered by the Aeronautics Branch of the D.O.C. which was empowered to regulate equipment, personnel, and the size of the field. The Branch was also charged with controlling the number of students assigned and hours flown each day by instructors. Flight instructors and aircraft would have to be licensed.

Only five flying schools were endorsed by the Department on July 15, 1929. Embry-Riddle was one of them.

An Airline, Too

Mr. Embry and Mr. Riddle embodied a philosophy that would become a tradition with Embry-Riddle. Once something was accomplished, they refused to be satisfied with the status quo. Instead, they looked for new horizons. One of those bold, new adventures was the subject of an April 15, 1929 headline in the Cincinnati *Commercial Tribune*:

EMBRY-RIDDLE TO BECOME LINK IN GIANT AIRWAYS

The founders of the School were determined to expand their operation, and they were not afraid to seek financial help from others.

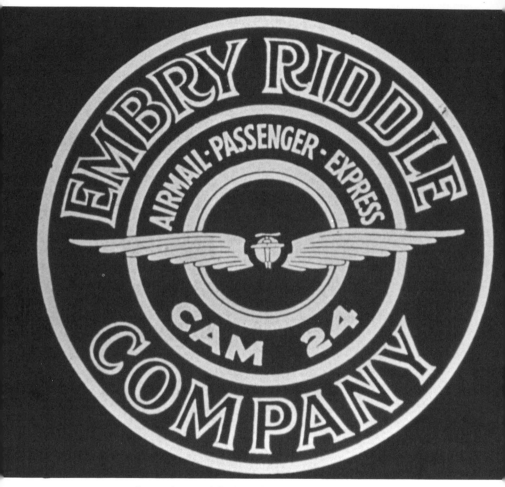

The Embry-Riddle logo left no doubt as to its mission.

From School to Airline

Embry and Riddle put up more than $10,000 of their own money, but more capital was needed to support the air mail services. Cincinnati businessmen contributed over $90,000, but this was still not enough.

Since the Company was a dealer for Fairchild Aircraft, Sherman Fairchild himself introduced Riddle to two highly respected New York investment banking firms—W. Averell Harriman & Company and Lehman Brothers. (Fairchild probably feared that the Company might sell other aircraft, such as the one offered by Glenn L. Curtiss, if he didn't help.)

Fairchild acted quickly and with insight. He appealed to the investors for assistance. They agreed, and created a new financial enterprise called "Aviation Corporation of Delaware" on March 1, 1929.

Stock was underwritten by W. Averell Harriman & Company and Lehman Brothers and offered for public sale at $17.50 per share. Some of the more optimistic friends of Embry and Riddle envisioned as much as $1 million in sales. To the amazement of everyone, nearly two million shares were sold immediately, raising $35 million in cash.

Other aviation companies were added. The new organization was involved with aircraft manufacturing, engine development, sales, schools, and air passenger service.

On April 15, 1929, Embry-Riddle filed a charter of incorporation naming T. Higbee Embry as President and J. Paul Riddle as Vice President. By creating the corporation as a holding company, Embry-Riddle received the capital it needed. The Aviation Corporation of Delaware issued the stock, but the control of the operation remained with Embry and Riddle.

With the added cash, Embry and Riddle began a venture that was ahead of its time—even for them. They laid the groundwork for a unique concept called an "air university." The theory was that a primary school would train new recruits, while a "university" that specialized in advanced commercial aviation would provide professional aviators.

The new Embry-Riddle Aviation Corporation had earlier

One of Embry-Riddle's pioneer instructors.

acquired Norton Field of Columbus, Ohio and the Columbus Flying Service. Later it purchased the Portsmouth (Ohio) Flying Service. If these were successful, future plans included opening schools in other Ohio cities.

The interest by potential enrollees was less than spectacular. Riddle attempted to gain more through advertisements and promotions, but nothing worked.

"Everybody was putting in schools everywhere," he said. "Our idea of an 'air university' never made it past the planning stage, I'm afraid."

The Embry-Riddle Company continued operating in Cincinnati as a subsidiary of the Aviation Corporation of Delaware, which was to become known as "AVCO." By the end of 1929, it controlled 81 different companies representing various aviation enterprises. Unfortunately, profits did not match its rapid growth.

The Corporation had lost $1.4 million. That was not much by today's standards, but in the Depression-dominated economy it was simply more red ink than its management could tolerate.

Routes of the acquired air transport system did not connect effectively. "It was simply a mess," says Mr. Riddle. Often cutthroat competition for passengers between the mail and non-mail subsidiaries resulted in everyone losing money.

A new, super holding company had to be organized in 1930. This new subsidiary of the Aviation Corporation of Delaware was called "American Airways."

Embry-Riddle, then, was directly involved with the emergence of two of aviation's most powerful industries— AVCO, and what today is known as "American Airlines." Yet in spite of the financial clout of these corporate giants, Embry-Riddle never took a back seat in corporate influence.

An Interlude

Embry and Riddle were still influential, respected authorities to whom the organization listened. Nonetheless, in

The Embry-Riddle staff in 1929.

terms of financial structure, the writing was on the wall. Reorganization was inevitable. Perhaps due to the fact that they had survived when others had counted them out, Embry and Riddle, so claim some historians, stubbornly refused to sell their stock and attempted for nearly one full year to ride out this latest storm. According to the same writers, the Embry-Riddle Company reluctantly bowed to the obvious and sold its stock to American Airways in return for shares of common stock in the airline.

Mr. Riddle, however, tells a different story. "We were running most of the operations of the airline part of the Aviation Corporation, he says. "We eventually sold our stock to the Aviation Corporation Airways in return for shares of common stock in the Corporation. It was simply a good deal for us all around."

By agreement, Embry-Riddle maintained control of its own operating company. Its 270-mile route had become a part of the Aviation Corporation's aviation empire, providing it with an important midwestern link in the network of this growing airline.

Eventually, all the subsidiaries of American Airways were dissolved. Thus, one of the sadder headlines in the history of aviation appeared in the *Air Transportation* Magazine on September 30, 1930:

EMBRY-RIDDLE CLOSES DOWN OLDEST SCHOOL

The School's closing marked the end of a pioneering organization as well as the entrepreneurial partnership of T. Higbee Embry and J. Paul Riddle.

Mr. Embry moved to California, where the exuberant businessman lived until his death in 1946.

Mr. Riddle went to New York, then to Dallas as a trouble-shooter in helping to structure the new organization. The corporate office was moved to St. Louis in March, 1932, merging with the Universal Division to be called the "Central Division of American Airways." In less than one year, the energetic but cautious aviator J. Paul Riddle left St. Louis and

Loading an Embry-Riddle airplane with mailsacks was a daily ritual at Lunken Field in Cincinnati.

the airline to seek his fortune in Florida. The man who had already become an aviation legend was only 32 years old.

The Embry-Riddle Company's association with Lunken Airport and its love affair with Cincinnati was now history. An era had passed; another was yet to be born.

3

World War II

The Aviation Building. The Technical Division occupied the entire former hotel from 1940 to 1944, and the school returned from 1952 to 1965. It was known as the "$1 Million Chicken Coop" for its use before 1940 and was demolished in May 1971 to make room for a juvenile court and youth hall.

"The growth and progress of the Riddle Technical School here as well as its importance in the national defense setup is remarkable." —Miami Daily News, 1941

John Paul Riddle didn't move to retire or to bask in the Miami sunshine. He saw a rich future for aviation in Florida. He was convinced, in fact, that Miami could develop into a major gateway to South America.

Shortly after he established permanent residence in Florida, Riddle formed the Palm Beach Aero Corporation. This latest venture had a modest beginning, but gained support from some local influential aviation enthusiasts such as Marshall "Doc" Rinker, Jake Boyd, and Paul Butler. In addition, Mr. Riddle formed the Miami Aero Corporation and the Florida Aero Corporation. All three served as foundations for his future endeavors.

In October 1939, Riddle formed an equal partnership with John G. McKay, a prominent Florida attorney and a former Army Air Corps lieutenant. Together they established a seaplane operation which they named "The Embry-Riddle School of Aviation" along what is now MacArthur Causeway. Shortly thereafter, the School added another training center at Miami's Municipal Airport to train students in consortium with the University of Miami.

As a basis for further expansion, the School created "divisions" for various operations. Each had its own general manager, while Riddle served as President and McKay as Vice President and Legal Advisor.

Overseas, the sounds of war grew more intense. Hitler's armies goose-stepped into Poland. Suddenly, England became vulnerable. Across the Pacific, Japan was flexing its muscles, threatening to rule the Eastern world.

Two years before America's direct involvement with the war, Riddle (now fondly referred to as "Boss Riddle") and McKay prepared the School to train pilots and mechanics. Both men sided with Brig. Gen. William (Billy) Mitchell who predicted at his court-martial in 1925 that aviation would play an important role if America ever signed a declaration of war.

On Sunday morning, December 7, 1941, the entire nation knew just how right they were.

Cadet Training

The United States needed to train pilots and mechanics in a hurry, and turned to those who could help. The Embry-Riddle School was ready, and offered the services of its 390 employees, including 87 flight instructors.

The Army Air Corps entrusted Embry-Riddle along with other private schools with the primary training of cadets, while the Corps devoted its own fields to advanced training.

Britain's Royal Air Force, too, sought schools for its future pilots, and Embry-Riddle was awarded a contract to provide this training.

Paul Riddle and John McKay had already expanded their training sites to four satellite airfields.

Carlstrom Field in Arcadia, Florida was the largest under the Southeastern Air Corps Training Center of Maxwell

Carlstrom Field, near Arcadia, Florida. Formerly a major flying field for the U.S. Army, Carlstrom became the largest civilian training field and was operated by Embry-Riddle until its closing in 1945. Today it is the site of the G. Pierce Wood Memorial Hospital.

The first cadet to report in a Carlstrom was Frank Beeson, being greeted by Len Povey (far right), as a second cadet and another company official look on. Lieutenant Beeson was killed in action over New Guinea in July 1942.

Aircraft Overhaul Department at Carlstrom Field. One of three locations of the Aircraft and Engine Division, Carlstrom Field was kept busy. The other two locations were in Miami and Coral Gables. The division overhauled more than 3,000 engines, 700 aircraft, and 21,000 aeronautical instruments of the nation's war effort.

Field, Alabama. Unlike other military bases, this 1,300-acre, flat, dry field was no make-shift operation. It had a look of permanency. Hangars formed its outer rim; inside were barracks, an infirmary, mess hall, classrooms, recreational facilities, even the legendary swimming pool into which a cadet was thrown by his classmates upon completing his first solo flight.

Leonard J. Povey served as General Manager over the fastpaced program that provided instruction for 500 cadets at one time over a nine-week course that included 60 hours of flight.

Both American and British pilots were trained at Carlstrom. When the first wave of RAF cadets arrived, the Associated Press reported: "The eyes of 99 Britons lighted when they glimpsed the new $300,000 Riddle Aeronautical Institute, with its lines of trainer planes, modern barracks, swimming pool, and tennis courts. 'The Royal Air Force will turn green with envy when it hears about this,' exulted one cadet as he examined his quarters."

During World War II, one of the widely published demonstrations of patriotism was the result of Carlstrom's staff. In May 1943, *The American Pilot and Aircraftsman* Magazine published "Carlstrom Field's Twelve Ways to Aid Hitler":

1. Griping about food.
2. Taking ground school lightly, thinking if you can fly a plane that is all you need.
3. Ground-looping through carelessness, resulting in time lost in plane repair.
4. Goldbricking in physical training, passing up the opportunity to develop strength, endurance, ability, and recreation.
5. Reporting to sick call with acute "drillitis" to evade duties that instill personal discipline so important to the fighting man.
6. Using open post to undo physical benefits of training.

Riddle Field, south of Lake Okeechobee. Here the company trained RAF pursuit and bomber pilots in primary and advanced flying from 1941 to 1945. The field is now the Airglades Airport.

RAF graduation at Riddle Field. Pictured is the cadet formation for one of many graduation days of pilots trained for the Royal Air Force by Embry-Riddle instructors. More than 2,000 RAF cadets stood proudly as they won their wings at Riddle Field. Biplanes stand to the rear of the formation, and advanced trainers are in the distance.

7. Failure to observe general rules of military courtesy. Save the chip on the shoulder for Adolf.
8. Poor use of time when you might be writing home. Your folks want to know how you are and their spirits must be kept up as much as yours.
9. Giving up if you are disqualified for further flight training. Remember, chickens don't fly, but they are darned useful birds.
10. Letting foresight sag. You will have your chance to fight, but you have to make good here first.
11. Losing your faith in worship. An hour in church might give you a fresher outlook for the week.
12. Forgetting there are several million more just like us in this war.

Riddle Field, a 2,500-acre site located at Clewiston, Florida, was the site of the No. 5 British Flying Training School and could accommodate 250 cadets. Used primarily for RAF training, it provided primary, basic, and advanced phases of flight instruction.

Operating as the "Riddle-McKay Aero College" Division, Embry-Riddle provided complete training for bomber and pursuit planes, including combat maneuvers, under the watchful eyes of General Manager G. Willis Tyson.

Dorr Field, like Carlstrom—also operating under the "Riddle Aeronautical Institute" Division—was located near Arcadia. Flight training began here before the end of summer 1941; by the New Year, cadets moved into the dormitories.

Embry-Riddle Field, near Union City, Tennessee, contained 870 acres, and was assigned to the "Riddle-McKay Aero Institute of Tennessee" Division. H. Roscoe Brinton, the first General Manager, initially guided the primary flight training for 100 cadets of the Army Air Corps.

The Seaplane Base in Miami became increasingly important, as it was one of the few places where Navy pilots could receive the basics in this specialized type of training. Among the students who earned their seaplane ratings here was one

Dorr Field, near Arcadia, Florida. Many Army Air Corps cadets began their training here, a site that is now a maximum security prison.

young officer from Huntsville, Tennessee who later distinguished himself in politics as a United States Senator. His name was Howard Baker, Jr.

Prior to the attack on Pearl Harbor, the Miami Landplane Base at Chapman Field located south of Miami on Biscayne Bay trained young men from both the civilian ranks and from the Civil Pilot Training Program [CPTP]—a project of the Civil Aeronautics Administration [CAA] to prepare college students as pilot reserves in the event of war. "One of our best instructors there was Tine Davis," says Mr. Riddle, "who could fly anything with wings." Mr. Davis, who later became one of the founders of the popular Winn-Dixie stores, remained a cherished friend and benefactor of Embry-Riddle throughout his entire life.

In the spring of 1940, one person changed the image that flying was a "for men only" career. Dorothy Ashe, daughter of the University of Miami's President, B.F. Ashe, was Embry-Riddle's first woman pilot to solo under the CPTP. Others followed. In less than a year, the School hired Helen Cavis—one of the 160 women in the United States who held a commercial certificate—as its first woman flight instructor.

Miss Cavis was originally hired not only to teach women pilots, but men as well.

Not everyone applauded this turn of events. Some had a hard time accepting the idea of a woman working in the previously male-dominated environment of aviation. One of the more brazen cadets was even bold enough to approach Mr. Riddle in his office, complaining that "no women— 'schoolmarms,'" as he and some of his companions called them—"should pilot an airplane."

"Bah!" retorted Riddle. "Any fool realizes that a plane doesn't care who's at the controls. Besides, in my opinion she flies a lot better than most of the men here . . . including you." Tilting his head and raising one bushy eyebrow, Riddle asked: "Is that what's really bothering you, young man?"

The red-faced cadet made an abrupt "about face" and left without saying another word.

THE SKY IS HOME

The women must have done something right. By the end of 1942, the Seaplane Base became an all-women operation, run and staffed by women headed by Ruth Norton, its director.

Most of the pilots who graduated from the Embry-Riddle School soon flew the skies above territories with strange-sounding names, such as Saipan, Leipzig, and Iwo Jima.

And many never returned.

Technical Division

As the Government called for more pilots and airplanes, Riddle and McKay realized that mechanics and technicians would be needed to "keep 'em flying." Consequently, in November 1940, they leased the south wing of the "Old Fritz Hotel" on N.W. 27th Avenue and 32nd Street in Miami for ground school and technical instruction.

The hotel, dubbed by many as one of Miami's "white elephants," was built in 1925 as a sanitarian health hotel by millionaire Joachim Fritz. With the stock market crash on Wall Street in October 1929, many of its clientele no longer could afford this luxury. The five-story structure was forced to close its doors in 1930. It sat dormant for several years, until a poultryman decided to use it as a chicken hatchery. When Riddle and McKay selected the building as the School's technical training site, the students and faculty referred to it as the "Aviation Building." The citizens of Miami, however, had baptized it with a somewhat less complimentary title— "The One Million Dollar Chicken Coop."

Yet Riddle and McKay proved they could even transform a "white elephant chicken coop" into a useful entity.

The August 17, 1941 edition of the *Miami News* agreed:

> The growth and progress of the Riddle Technical School here as well as its importance in the national defense setup is remarkable. Its approximately 500 students from North and South America are studying all phases of aircraft, engineering, construction,

Both the U.S. and British flags flew over Embry-Riddle training fields during the war.

Cadets trained by Embry-Riddle prepare for flight at Carlstrom Field.

flight operation, and maintenance. More than 1,000 skilled craftsmen, men and boys with little or no previous aircraft experience, will be turned out here this year to join scores of other graduates working in aircraft plants all over the country.

The Technical Division operated seven days and five evenings a week. In 1942, the Army sent more trainees. The School tripled its training schedule, and classes were taught 24 hours a day, seven days a week. The concentrated program of study produced trained technicians, sometimes after only six months of classes.

As rapidly as students completed their courses of study, there were still not enough men to fill all the vacancies in the work force. To fill these gaps, the School opened its technical courses to female students in 1942. The women were taught and performed all types of work within limitations of their physical strength.

Each student learned by "doing" as much as through textbooks. The highly individualized method of training included a personal instructor who guided the student step-by-step through every phase of maintenance.

Unique demands required unique training methods. In some instances, students had to learn to work by touch alone, for on the fighting fronts they would have to work in total darkness.

There were no semesters, no summer vacations, nor a lot of the other things normally associated with today's institutions of higher education. Only when the instructor cleared him, and the student successfully passed his exams, was he ready to work at an airplane factory or hangar.

One of those aircraft plants was a part of Embry-Riddle's Overhaul Division created in July 1942 on 20th Street in Miami, a short drive from the Aviation Building. The *Fly Paper*—the official in-house publication of Embry-Riddle— described the fast-paced activity: "In a hangar at the back of the Aviation Building, engines for overhaul are received at one end of the building . . . pass through a production line procedure . . . and, a few hours later, pop out of the other end of the building completely overhauled and ready for service, including even the required 'run in' in the engine test house."

The major problems confronting this new division included obtaining tools, equipment, and personnel. Tools and equipment often had to be designed and manufactured by the instructors; women provided the solution to the personnel problems. In fact, by June 1943, women constituted more than one-third of the division's employees.

The School also set up an Instrument Department in suburban Coral Gables in which technicians repaired and refinished all types of aircraft instruments.

Since many of the potential students were from South America, Riddle and McKay offered dual-language instruction. As a result, the School created a partial translation of aircraft nomenclature into Spanish and Portuguese—one of the first such authoritative works ever attempted.

A contract was awarded to Embry-Riddle through the CAA to participate in the Inter-American Aviation Training Program.

The first 70 students from Latin America arrived in January. In just seven months, 21 students from nine countries completed their courses of study.

Embry-Riddle trained men and women throughout the course of World War II, until August 6, 1945, when a 29-year-old Air Corps Colonel, Paul Tibbets, flew the *Enola Gay* over Hiroshima and gave the order to drop an experimental bomb that not only ended the War, but also changed the course of history.

Transition

By the time General Douglas MacArthur signed the peace treaty on September 2nd aboard the *U.S.S. Missouri,* more than 26,000 men and women had earned their wings or technical licenses through Embry-Riddle. Through all of this,

The Seaplane Base in Miami was a training are for many military pilots during the War.

the School's remarkable record of safety won the praises of every branch of the Armed Services.

In addition, the Aircraft and Engine Division overhauled more than 3,000 engines and 700 aircraft. The Instrument Department in Coral Gables repaired and refinished at least 21,000 aeronautical instruments.

For the war-time programs, the School successfully trained students for the fighting fronts. It was only fitting that it would now prepare to equip students equally well for a world at peace.

★★★★★★★★★ ★ ★ ★★

4

Toward a University

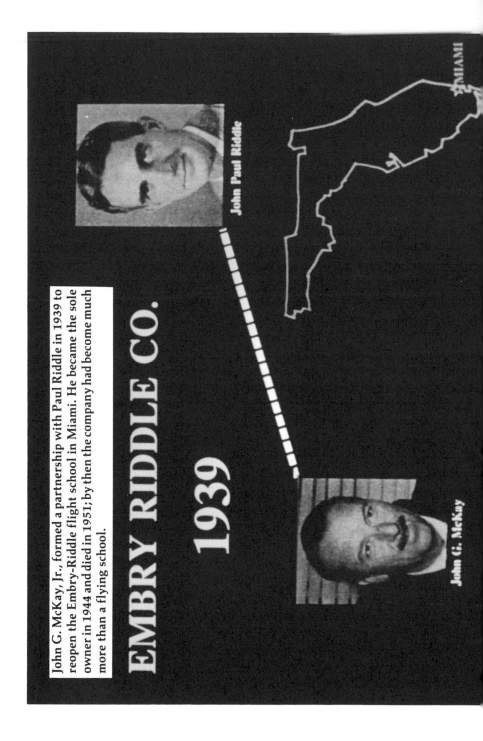

John G. McKay, Jr., formed a partnership with Paul Riddle in 1939 to reopen the Embry-Riddle flight school in Miami. He became the sole owner in 1944 and died in 1951; by then the company had become much more than a flying school.

EMBRY RIDDLE CO.
1939

John Paul Riddle

John G. McKay

MIAMI

"Be it resolved that J.R. Hunt be, and he hereby is, elected president of Embry-Riddle Aeronautical Institute, at a salary of $900 per month, to serve at the pleasure of the Board."
—Minutes from the Board of Trustees,
September 3, 1963

Changing of the Guard

"It was the hardest decision in my life, but it's something I had to do," said John Paul Riddle when he sold his interest in the School to John McKay in September 1944. Over the past 18 years, Mr. Riddle had carved a niche for himself in the history of aviation.

Most men, we suppose, would be satisfied. But John Paul Riddle was not like most men. He was not running away from a challenge; he was setting his sights on a new one. The *Fly Paper* put the story into a nutshell: "John Paul Riddle is leaving now for ventures in a new world, the world of aviation fast developing in neighboring Brazil. There he found the same sky, the same air, but new horizons, far reaching and, as yet, unconquered. There are new dreams to come true."

Those new dreams included the "Escola Tecnica de Aviacao" [Technical School of Aviation] in Sao Paulo, which began as a cooperative venture involving Embry-Riddle and the Brazilian Air Ministry.

73

The new school in Brazil was the result of a suggestion by Mr. Peter Ordway, a graduate of Embry-Riddle and former Dean of Students and Advertising Director. "Peter Ordway was so supportive of Embry-Riddle that when his son was born, he "pre-enrolled" the infant for the freshman class eighteen years later," says Mr. Riddle.

Heading the operations in Brazil were David Beatty, who would later gain fame as a backer for several motion pictures at M.G.M., and William Lehman, a long-time friend and former instructor for Mr. Riddle.

After Riddle dissolved his partnership with McKay, the Brazilian school was no longer a part of Embry-Riddle. Riddle remained with it, nurtured it to prosperity, then turned it over to the Brazilian Government. In just three years, the institution graduated 3,500 students; at one time, it employed 650 North American instructors.

Back in Miami, Embry-Riddle was beginning a series of transformations, including two name changes and three moves.

The Embry-Riddle International School of Aviation, as it was now called, consisted of the Technical School in Coral Gables; the Flight Division, with two bases at MacArthur Causeway and Chapman Field, now devoted to training pilots for commercial and business aviation; and the Aircraft Division at N.W. 20th Street and Chapman Field.

The military no longer needed private schools to teach its pilots and mechanics. The new market was civilian training, although the School signed contracts with the Veterans Administration to instruct those qualified under the G.I. Bill of Rights and with the Free French Republic to provide advanced flight training for its naval cadets.

John McKay became the new President of the School, appointed new officers, and laid the groundwork for the new challenges of the postwar era.

New Settings

All divisions of Embry-Riddle moved to the Opa-Locka

Early recruitment efforts. The Embry-Riddle School of Aviation searched for students interested in civil aviation.

THE SKY IS HOME

Airport in October 1947. The Airport, built by Glenn Curtiss and enlarged by the Navy during World II, provided all the spaces necessary for the Flight and Technical Schools. A large Navy-constructed hangar, an adjacent hangar, and a utility building were used by the School. The approximately 400 students who enrolled over the next few years utilized the dormitories and cafeteria at the airport.

During the Korean War, the School was once again called upon by the military to train mechanics. The nation's newest branch of service, the United States Air Force, contracted with Embry-Riddle to train airmen in the fundamentals of airplane maintenance, from the basic instructions on how to care for hand tools to the complex principles of aerodynamics, electronics, and hydraulics. More than 1,500 Air Force recruits trained at Opa-Locka during a 16 month period.

The geography was different, but the tradition continued. Embry-Riddle insisted on rigid adherence to safety standards. "The School enjoys a high safety record," reported the *Air Trails* Magazine of November 1948. "Correct flying habits and a sound foundation on the ground to sharpen efficiency in the air is a 'must' for the beginner or the commercial pilot seeking additional ratings."

John McKay ran the School, making most of the major decisions until, suddenly, he died in 1951. Mrs. Isabel McKay, his widow, who had served as his assistant since 1945, assumed the Presidency. She thus became the only woman to head an aviation school in the United States.

For one so wrapped-up in all phases of aviation, it might be assumed that Mrs. McKay was an avid pilot. "Not really," she confessed to a reporter for the *Miami Herald*. "I started taking flying lessons once, but gave it up after only four hours in the air."

In 1952 the Marine Corps occupied the Opa-Locka Airport and forced the School to relocate once again. This time the officers, classrooms, and shops were moved back to the "Aviation Building" (still called the "Chicken Coop" by most

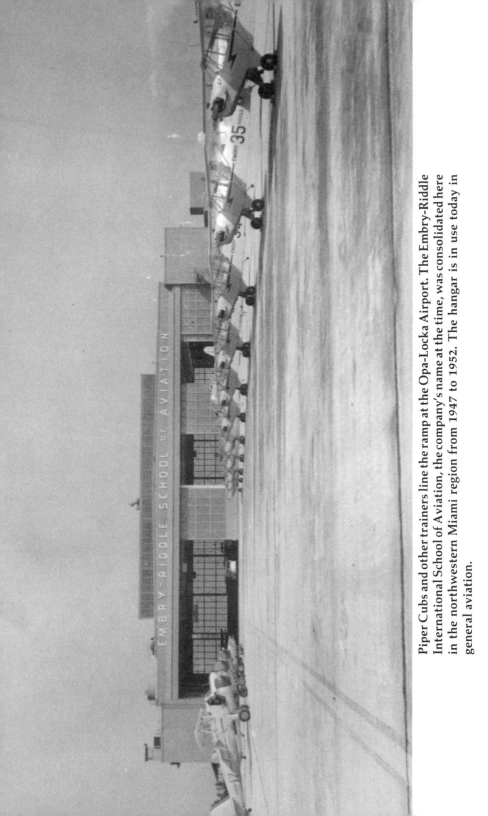

Piper Cubs and other trainers line the ramp at the Opa-Locka Airport. The Embry-Riddle International School of Aviation, the company's name at the time, was consolidated here in the northwestern Miami region from 1947 to 1952. The hangar is in use today in general aviation.

THE SKY IS HOME

people), while the Flight School operated out of the Tamiami Airport, eight miles away.

While at Tamiami, the School renewed its consortium with the University of Miami. The two schools combined to provide students with the necessary requirements for a four-year degree in Aviation Administration and a two-year certificate in the Business Pilot Program. Four years later, Embry-Riddle provided flight training for the University's Air Force ROTC students.

Non-Profit Status

Embry-Riddle's enrollment increased steadily over the next few years due to the lure of aviation for students not only in America, but throughout the world. The School's enrollment read like a roster at the United Nations. There were young men from China, Turkey, Lebanon, Israel, Egypt, Pakistan, Norway, Belgium, Switzerland, England, Bermuda, Cuba, Trinidad, Canada, Columbia, Bolivia, Honduras, Venezuela, Guatemala, and Panama.

It was this world-wide appeal, in fact, that enabled Embry-Riddle to continue operating. Despite all efforts to promote the Institute within the Miami Community, the School was better known outside its own hometown. By 1958, the 1,000 students represented 44 states and 21 foreign countries.

Aviation had reached the jet age. If Embry-Riddle was going to serve the industry, it had to adjust. "We are keeping pace with aviation developments by including a study in jet theory, and we will offer courses in jet engines in the near future," promised Mrs. McKay.

The School, now named "Embry-Riddle Aeronautical Institute," offered courses for jet specialists and electronics technicians. With this more sophisticated curriculum, there were, of course, greater expenses for the day-to-day operation.

Until now, nearly every dollar of Embry-Riddle's income came directly from student tuition. If the Institute were to survive, other sources of support had to be generated. One

On the death of her husband in 1951, Mrs. Isabel McKay became the president and general manager of Embry-Riddle. She reorganized the company in 1961 as a non-profit school, appointed Jack Hunt her successor in 1963, and remained as a member of the Board until her death in 1972.

Jack Reed Hunt was the president from September 1963 until his death in January 1984.

way was to gain acceptance as an independent, non-profit institution.

After more than a year of lobbying through persuasive rhetoric, Mrs. McKay, Paul Freedland, and other Board members were successful in winning approval from the State of Florida to grant non-profit status to the Institute. On September 1, 1961, it could receive financial assistance from philanthropic organizations and, if necessary, even from the Government.

New Faces

Mrs. McKay continued serving as President until she was certain that the Institute would function smoothly. By New Year's Day, 1962, she demonstrated that confidence when she turned over the reins to G. Ross Henninger. Mrs. McKay became Chairman of the Board of Trustees.

Mrs. McKay's faith in Mr. Henninger's ability to lead the Institute may have been misguided. For a variety of reasons, the arrangement simply did not work out. Mrs. McKay knew it; the Board knew it. On June 4 of that year Mrs. McKay called for a special meeting of the Board.

"This is a sad day for me and for Embry-Riddle," she said. "I must ask that you, the members of the Board, remove Mr. Heninnger as President."

Mr. Henninger, however, protested this motion, and appealed to the Board for support.

After heated debate, the Board voted unanimously either to accept the resignation of President Henniger, or, if he refused to resign, to terminate him.

Mr. Henninger resigned.

A long-time friend of the Institute, Dr. Grover Noetzel, accepted the role as interim President while the Board searched for a new leader.

On September 3, 1963, the Board announced that it had found that leader.

Mrs. McKay read the official pronouncement: "BE IT

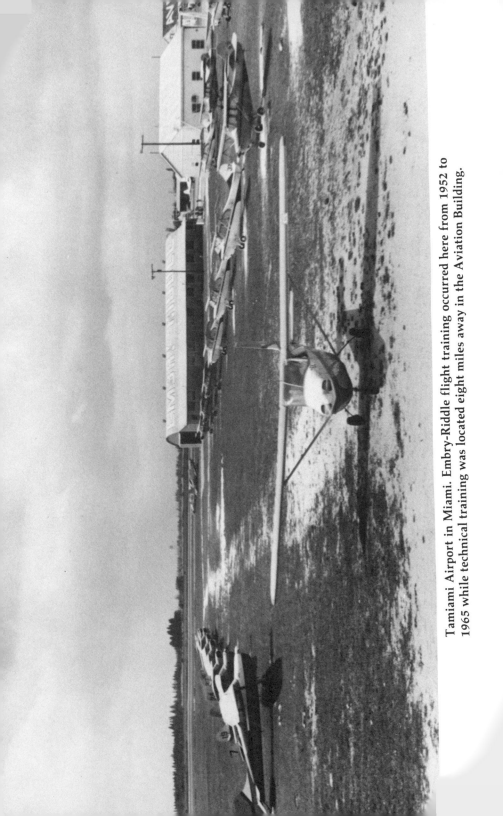

Tamiami Airport in Miami. Embry-Riddle flight training occurred here from 1952 to 1965 while technical training was located eight miles away in the Aviation Building.

Loading up for Daytona. Some of the thirty-four trucks enlisted by the Daytona Beach Jaycees can be seen loading up at the Tamiami Airport to haul the Embry-Riddle Aeronautical Institute to its new home.

RESOLVED that J. R. Hunt be, and he hereby is, elected President of Embry-Riddle Aeronautical Institute at a salary of $900 per month to serve at the pleasure of the Board."

Jack Reed Hunt had worked with the Institute since June of that year as an administrative assistant to Mrs. McKay. Hunt, a dashing former Navy commander, had gained international fame as the pilot of the first non-stop, round-trip flight across the Atlantic in the U.S. Navy blimp ZPG-2. Hunt led the 14-man crew of the airship *Snowbird* for 364.2 hours over 9,448 miles from March 4 to 16, 1957. The route took them from Massachusetts to Portugal, to Africa, to Puerto Rico, to Cuba, to Florida. It was the longest non-refueled sustained flight ever made.

For this feat, Fleet Admiral William F. "Bull" Halsey awarded Commander Hunt the Distinguished Flying Cross. President Dwight D. Eisenhower presented him with the Harmon Trophy at a special ceremony in the Oval Office of the White House.

Soon after he was discharged from the service, Hunt established a solid reputation as a real estate investor. One of the reasons for his success was his unusual ability to recognize the value of certain properties that escaped others.

Jack Hunt didn't have to wait long for an opportunity to prove what sort of leader he would be. Within a few weeks, the Dade County Port Authority announced that the Tamiami Airport would be phased out of existence. Embry-Riddle had to find a new home.

Selecting a Site

Transporting a school can produce some nearly insurmountable problems. The most obvious is the physical transporting of equipment, books, and machinery from one location to another. Add to these the fact that the holdings included several aircraft, the problem becomes even greater.

Other questions had to be answered as well. What effect would the move have on recruiting students? Would this affect the retention of the faculty and staff? How would accrediting agencies view the move?

"Embry-Riddle is virtually unknown in Dade County," said President Hunt to the Board in January 1964, "yet, internationally, the School enjoys a fine reputation."

Hunt and the Board developed a plan of attack. Instead of fighting the apathy of Miami, it would move the institute elsewhere.

Twenty-two sites were visited by officials. Each one offered certain advantages. However, holding the most promise were five Florida locations: Sebring, Fort Pierce, Plant City, Dade County (outside of Miami), and Daytona Beach.

Embry-Riddle suddenly found itself in a new role. All five communities really wanted the Institute. Daytona Beach fought harder than the others.

Led by Gary Cunningham, a bold entrepreneur who had gained a reputation for getting what he went after, the Daytona Beach "Committee of One Hundred"—a group of citizens dedicated to invite new business into the area— pledged its support not only to roll out the welcome mat, but aid in the actual moving of the campus 250 miles north.

Daytona Beach

"This is a victory for the good image of the Daytona Beach area," reported the Daytona Beach *Evening News* on April 27, 1965.

Moving a family or a small business from one locale to another is expensive; moving an entire institute of this magnitude could be financially prohibitive. Were it not for organizations such as the Daytona Beach Jaycees, the "Committee of One Hundred," and local residents willing to donate time and energy into transporting everything north, the move to the Daytona Beach area could never have been accomplished.

Underwriting the costs of the move was no small challenge. The School's accountant put a sharp pencil to paper

Hunt the Mover. Jack Hunt (left) helps to load one of the trucks bound for Daytona Beach.

and determined that it needed $75,000 before the first library book could be packed.

Vice President of the "Committee of 100" was Philip H. Elliott, Jr., a prominent attorney of Daytona Beach, who later would be selected as the school's legal representative and member of its Board of Trustees. He was one of the first to support the project.

But his faith was not shared by everyone. Elliott recalls: "Most of the community leaders showed little enthusiasm for the move. Some bluntly asked, 'How can they be an asset to the area if they have to borrow money just to move in?' "

Gary Cunningham turned to a young, aggressive insurance executive, John C. "Jay" Adams, to serve as chairman for the drive. Together, they knocked on doors of local business owners and interested citizens. "This will be a loan, not a gift," both Cunningham and Adams promised.

Whether it was the community's confidence in the Institute or in both men that determined the response is debatable. Nevertheless, every dime of the $75,000 was raised in just four days.

A convoy of trucks and drivers was organized. On April 24, 56 volunteers met at 7:30 a.m. at the Daytona Beach Airport, climbed aboard 34 donated trucks and vans, and drove south on U.S. Route 1 toward Miami.

Throughout that afternoon and evening, the crew loaded each book and piece of equipment belonging to the Institute aboard the vehicles. By 3:00 a.m., the final rope was secured. Most of the volunteers slept in the trucks until sunrise. Slowly the vans pulled away.

After nine hours, the convoy chugged into the Daytona Beach Airport only 30 minutes behind schedule to a welcoming party unlike that ever imagined by the exhausted crew.

"It was a royal welcome," remembers Cunningham. "Scores of Jaycees and others cheered our caravan as we drove up Midway Road. We were tired, hot, sweating, and unkempt. We must have looked like bums, but they greeted us like conquering heroes. When I got out of the truck, one of

"Operation Bootstrap." Thirty-four heavily loaded trucks make a convoy on the return drive to Daytona Beach early on the second day of the operation. More than fifty volunteers went along to help.

them handed me a cold beer. That was the best damned beer I've ever had in my life."

When the last empty bottle was tossed in the trash can, no one could deny that "Operation Bootstrap," as they called it, was an unqualified success. The entire operation—lock, stock, and airplane—was transported without a scratch from Miami to Daytona Beach.

Original plans called for Embry-Riddle to relocate to the Ormond Beach Municipal Airport about 10 miles north of the heart of Daytona Beach. As a temporary set-up, however, Jack Hunt and his staff leased temporary quarters at the Daytona Beach Airport and planned to operate there, while the permanent campus was constructed in Ormond Beach along the Tomoka River.

The School concluded operations in Miami in April. One month later, it opened its doors for classes in Daytona Beach. Its total assets were a half million dollars' worth of equipment, a determined administration, and the whole-hearted support of a progressive community.

During its nearly 40 years of operation, Embry-Riddle trained nearly 40,000 students. But even this was only a prelude to what would happen in Daytona Beach.

5

Growing Pains

Shown here is the flight line at the Daytona Beach Municipal Airport about 1966. The hangar in left-center had been hauled from the Tamiami Airport by another company.

"With all this building came unexpected expenses. We were literally at the bottom of the financial barrel."
—Jack R. Hunt, 1966

Building Boom

The Embry-Riddle Aeronautical Institute opened its doors for classes in Daytona Beach on May 19, 1965, Mr. Riddle's birthday and 39 years after the Embry-Riddle Flying School offered that first flying lesson in Cincinnati.

The Institute was divided into three divisions—the College of Engineering, the Airframe and Powerplant Technician School, and the Flight School. Enrollment that summer term numbered 239, including the 168 students who relocated from Miami.

The Institute operated at the Daytona Beach Municipal Airport in five leased buildings. The "Naval Reserve Building" contained the College of Engineering on the upper floor, and part of the Airframe and Powerplant School on the ground floor. Administrative offices were located in the "Army Reserve Building." A third building off Midway Avenue housed more of the Airframe and Powerplant

School. The dormitory was half of a city-owned building shared with the Kansas City Athletics Baseball Club.

The Flight School and remainder of the Airframe and Powerplant School were at a hangar leased from the Daytona Beach Aviation, Inc. The 9,600-square-foot hangar had been hauled from the Tamiami Airport by Daytona Beach Aviation, which added another 5,760 square feet to it.

"With all this building came unexpected expenses. We were literally at the bottom of the financial barrel," recalled President Hunt. "There was only one thing to do if we hoped to survive. Five trustees and myself signed personal notes for five thousand dollars so that the next payroll could be made."

Their faith paid off. Five hundred fifteen students registered for fall classes.

"Now our problem was not *can* we grow, but how fast can we *afford* to grow,"said President Hunt with a sigh of relief.

The increasing enrollment proved both a blessing and a curse. One year later, when the student body reached 750, the School had more students than it could handle with existing facilities. An additional 20 airplanes were leased. After unsuccessfully attempting to persuade the City to relocate the Kansas City Athletics, the School used four local hotels to house 300 students.

Buildings had to be added in order to keep up with the influx of students. In February, two prefabricated buildings were set up and were used as a library and a combination student center/ book-store. They were erected near the Naval Reserve Building.

The City leased to Embry-Riddle a 1.5 acre site west of the Terminal on which the School constructed a hangar large enough to include four much-needed classrooms.

The enrollment reached 1,015 students the next fall. More dormitory space was needed promptly. The School leased a new apartment complex (now the Alhambra Apartments) on Nova Road for 287 students, and purchased the Mount Vernon Motor Lodge on South Ridgewood for 40 more students.

Growing Pains

Progress toward the permanent campus in Ormond Beach had come to a screeching halt. Disagreements arose between Embry-Riddle and the City officials as to how large the School could grow.

Jack Hunt had many virtues, but patience was not one of them. "It was either put up or shut up," he said. "They shut up, so we simply quit wasting each other's time."

One month later, Embry-Riddle had its permanent home. The school arranged with Daytona Beach for use of an 85-acre tract in the northeast section of the Airport. By this agreement, Embry-Riddle agreed to purchase the property for $42,500 per acre, plus pay $50,000 for water and sewerage preparation. In addition, it was allowed to purchase the land piecemeal over the next three years.

"There was no question about it. Daytona Beach wanted us to stay where we were," said President Hunt.

The next few months were saturated with building and phenomenal growth.

The first shovel of dirt was turned on October 17, 1967 for a new 386-student dormitory.

Every penny of the $75,000 loaned by local residents toward the move was repaid within only 19 months.

The faculty and staff increased from 38 to 180. The annual payroll was $860,000, and the economic impact on the community surpassed $2,500,000.

More buildings were financed by federal loans, federal grants, private donations, and school income. One of the more "radical" designs was named the new "Academic Complex."

The original drawings proposed rectangular buildings.

"Not flexible enough," said President Hunt. "Conventional buildings waste too much gawd-dang space." He went on to explain that a rectangular building loses up to 25 percent to corridors, stairways, and storage areas. A hexagonal design, on the other hand, loses only 10 percent.

Hunt's ability to persuade was demonstrated when three

First classrooms in Daytona. This structure was known as the Naval Reserve Building at the Daytona Beach Airport, where Embry-Riddle held its first classes in 1965.

hexagonal buildings connected by covered walks were erected east of the Airport.

The buildings didn't appear by magic, although some might consider it a miracle that Embry-Riddle was able to raise the necessary 1.3 million dollars necessary. Once again, "Jay" Adams was asked to spearhead a local campaign for $325,000—a necessary requirement before any matching or government funds were awarded. In order to meet this quota, Adams had to put his signature on a personally-secured promissory note in order to generate the needed cash.

Due to the ever increasing student enrollment, classes were actually conducted in the new "Academic Complex" in February 1969, although the building was not completed until the fall.

The Flight Line reflected the fact that the Institute was growing faster than anticipated. It was a mixed breed of types and color schemes, including Cessna 150s, Piper Cherokees, single-engine Aero Commanders, three classic twin-engine Beech B-18S, plus a blue and yellow Stearman biplane rebuilt by some of the students.

In 1968, Embry-Riddle reorganized, and purchased another eight acres of land. The groundwork was laid for recognition as a major institution of higher education. That same year, it received accreditation from the Southern Association of Schools and Colleges [SACS].

The granting of accreditation did not come easy. Jack Hunt appeared before the SACS assembly of delegates in December 1968 with a mission to convince them that Embry-Riddle was more than a glorified flight school. He introduced to the assembly his concept of a "University of the Air." He explained that Embry-Riddle was pioneering a new concept in flight training which involved a second student pilot riding along in the back seat of a training flight as an observer.

The unique training system was called the "1 + 1 Gemini-flight Technique." Hunt explained: "When a student is operating the controls, he often tends to worry more about what the airplane is doing and not what he is doing. Sitting in the back seat, however, he can learn from the mistakes being made by the student pilot at the controls. The next time they go up, they swap places, and the other student learns from his mistakes."

Hunt's argument was convincing primarily because he believed in what he was saying. On the many occasions he hosted a visitor on the campus, he pointed to a Piper Cherokee and exclaimed: "This is a classroom; it just happens to look llike an airplane."

Those who were at the SACS gathering testify that it was Jack Hunt's pride in Embry-Riddle's product that was most persuasive in winning approval for accreditation.

Financial woes again dominated the concerns of the Administration. "We were simply running out of cash and credit," says "Jay" Adams. Adams, who now served on the Board of Trustees and had earned a reputation in the community as one of the more vocal supporters of the School, tried in vain to get loans from area banks during the early fall of 1969. Not only was the School obligated to pay its debts for its rapid building program, but, unless it could get a quick infusion of cash, it could not meet the December payrolls for faculty and staff.

Jack Hunt reached into his bag of imaginative solutions and produced yet another unique idea. On November 15 he announced that any student who prepaid his next semester's tuition before the end of the current term could return to school on January 6; otherwise, he would have to report on January 2. Hunt hoped the extra four days vacation would be enough of an incentive to gather enough income to meet the immediate needs.

The plan worked. Faculty and staff were paid on time, and the School could get on with the business of education.

Progress came in the form not only of academic standing and building construction, but in other areas as well.

Until 1967, Embry-Riddle, like the rest of the aviation community, was dominated by men. Jack Hunt determined it

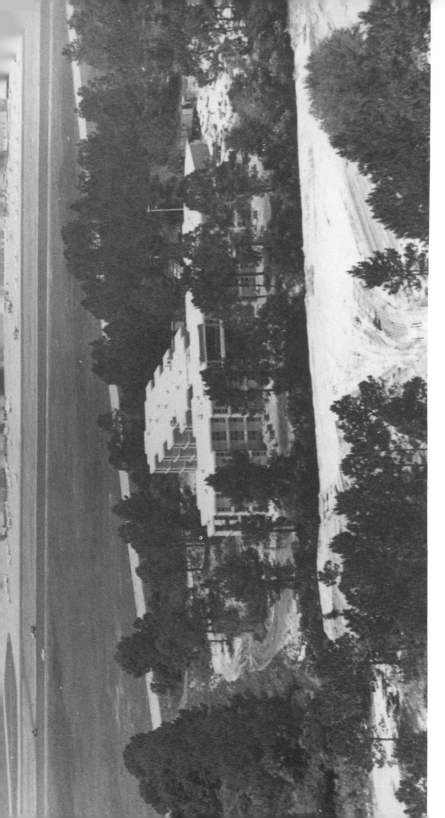

A dormitory for Daytona. Dorm I, the first permanent structure of Embry-Riddle in Daytona Beach, was built in 1968 to house 386 students.

was time to open the doors to female flying buffs. In the summer of '67, three co-eds—Penny Choranec, Linda Larsen, and Jackie Wimpy—formed the vanguard of what promised to be a rapidly expanding group once the word got around.

"There's a big future for women in aviation," predicted Hunt. "Of course, it's going to take a little longer to get them into the cockpit. It takes time for ideas to change."

The ideas eventually changed about a lot of things, including the academic status of the Institute.

Graduating to a University

The three divisions were dissolved, replaced by two colleges: The College of Aeronautical Studies and the College of Aviation Technology. The School's engineering courses had already been accredited by the Engineering Council for Professional Development; the Flight Program and Airframe/Powerplant Program had earned approval of the Federal Aviation Administration [FAA].

On June 9, 1970, the blue and gold sign at the entrance to the campus that welcomed visitors to Embry-Riddle Aeronautical Institute was repainted. In place of the word "Institute," was an even more impressive word—"University."

The impact of this superior academic identification attracted even more students. More buildings were constructed.

Ground was broken in April 1971 for another complex named in honor of Gill Robb Wilson, founder of the Civil Air Patrol and former editor of *Flying* magazine. The complex consisted of three pods, with the two-story structure later named the "Tine Davis Building," honoring one of the founders of the Winn-Dixie Food Stores, who was a benefactor of the University at times when financial support was an absolute necessity.

Amid all this growth Jack Hunt needed solid leadership at the helm of the Board of Trustees. One Board member who possessed the necessary leadership qualities was Brig. General William W. Spruance. In 1972, Hunt approached the General with a request to serve as Chairman.

"I don't know. I've never done this before," answered Spruance.

"Then take it temporarily," said Hunt.

"I will, until you find someone who knows what he is doing," joked Spruance.

The General has served as Chairman from that day until now.

During his 14 years as Chairman, Spruance and his fellow Board members tackled their share of problems—some of which divided the members into separate camps.

One of the more enthusiastic debates came early in 1972 when the School searched for an appropriate home for its President.

Austin O. Combs, a community leader, Board member, and successful realtor, was never afraid to meet a challenge head-on, and negotiated the purchase of a large, ocean-front home on A-1-A. Combs faced plenty of opposition from some Board members. "Some of them thought this was too much of a financial undertaking," says Combs. "But we were able to convince a majority of them to purchase the site. Today, it's worth many times the purchase price."

The President's Residence, better known as "The Battleship" because of its unusual silhouette, is the setting for community activities and receptions. Even the most severe skeptic admits it was one of Embry-Riddle's wisest investments.

On the Campus, the ramp constructed for the University's airplane fleet was dedicated January 19, 1974 with a unique ribbon-cutting ceremony. Students and faculty watched in awe as 72-year old John Paul Riddle, taxied a Cessna-172 through the ribbons onto the ramp.

It was a busy day for the participants who then walked to the site of the ground breaking for another new building— the "University Center."

Embry-Riddle students learn about aerodynamics through the wind tunnel.

Growing Pains

Construction on the first of the three buildings of the Aviation Maintenance Technology Center began in 1975 and was available for classes in 1977. It was none too soon. The number of students continued to grow; fall enrollment for '77 reached an astounding 2,725.

The Wind Tunnel had to be relocated to make room for airport expansion. The Engineering Technology Building, a prefabricated metal structure, was completed in 1978 to consolidate the aeronautical engineering program and house the wind tunnel.

That same year, the second dormitory was under construction, and the Tine Davis/Winn-Dixie Swimming Pool was completed.

In addition to the growth of buildings and academic offerings, the University sponsored both an Army and an Air Force ROTC program. The Air Force ROTC eventually grew to become the second largest detachment in the nation.

In 13 years, the campus in Daytona Beach grew to a stature never imagined by those sweating, tired volunteers of "Operation Bootstrap" who stepped from their trucks after their nine-hour drive from Miami. Even the July 2, 1979 issue of *Time* magazine referred to Embry-Riddle as "the Harvard of the Sky." Certainly, no one would blame the Administration for taking time out for a few bows.

Some people, however, are never satisfied with the status quo. And even Jack Hunt's closest friends didn't realize that he was eyeing further opportunities for growth.

★★ ★★★★★ ★★ ★★★ ★

6

Sixty Years Young

★★★★★★★★★★★★★★★★★★★★★★★★★★★

The Daytona campus in 1985. This aerial photograph shows the Daytona Beach campus buildings and other features. Clyde Morris Boulevard is at the top left. The famous speedway is in the foreground.

"Embry-Riddle doesn't belong to me or to the Board of Trustees. It belongs to everybody in the United States. And that, ladies and gentlemen, is a big responsibility."
— Jack R. Hunt, 1983

The Western Campus

"An opportunity such as this comes to us only once in a lifetime," said the visionary President Hunt to some members of the Board of Trustees in 1977. "Others consider it a lost cause," he continued. "For us, it's a chance to grow beyond all our former expectations.".

Jack Hunt was talking about a large campus nine miles north of Prescott, Arizona, once called "Prescott College."

The college had a less than spectacular history. Once an institution that offered courses such as "Wilderness Survival" and was noted for its "Outward Bound" program, the school went bankrupt in 1974. Its students were told about the school's demise through a cursory announcement on December 18 and ordered to clear out by midnight. The campus lay deserted until 1977, when Hunt, a few Trustees, and some administrators walked the 511-acre campus near the Prescott Municipal Airport.

"Can you imagine a Western Campus for Embry-Riddle out here? " asked Hunt.

The Prescott campus. The recreation facilities are in the foreground. The Classroom buildings and the library are beyond, among the trees. The dormitories are in the background.

"It seems to me that you already have," answered Dr. Ronald Wiley, one of the University deans.

Dr. Wiley, a psychologist, was correct in his analysis. At the persuasive urging of the President, the Board of Trustees voted in 1978 to purchase the property for a fraction of the assessed value.

The original plan was to establish a college preparatory school for eleventh and twelfth grade students, using flight as a motivation for academic performance. Within five years, the Trustees hoped to develop a four-year branch of the University at this site.

The college preparatory idea never gained acceptance by prospective students. Something else had to be done.

Jack Hunt and the Trustees acted quickly. The concept of a Western Campus was reclassified from "future plans" to "current project." Buildings were renovated; classrooms and office spaces were shaped from existing structures. By the fall of 1978, the campus opened its doors to 264 students and a small staff.

"The students could smell the fresh paint and sawdust as they were registering for classes," said General William Spruance, Chairman of the Board of Trustees, "but there was no mistake that we were here to stay."

Before the champagne corks were popped in celebration, President Hunt warned of one possible danger: "The Prescott Campus is a part of the one university. Each part of the University is the same as a member of a family. We cannot entertain a plan that will in any way weaken the whole, or we will destroy what we have worked so hard to build."

The Prescott Campus that year offered just one degree— a Bachelor of Science in Aeronautical Science. The limited facilities and the hastily assembled student body combined to create a need for unique programming.

Students were divided into two groups—the gold and blue. The blue group attended academic classes on Monday, Wednesdays, and Fridays, and flight line activities on Tuesdays, Thursdays and Saturdays. The gold group alternated schedules for academics and flight.

Seven full-time and three part-time instructors carried the academic load. Twenty-six flight instructors taught in 15 Grumman Tiger Cats.

Over the years, more buildings were remodeled. Student enrollments increased. The 1985 fall enrollment totaled 888; the staff numbered 160.

Prescott now offers six degrees, and its more sophisticated flight line includes eight Cessna 172s, one Cessna 172 with retractable landing gear, and two twin-engine Piper Seminoles.

Paul Daly, Chancellor of the Prescott Campus, promises continued growth both academically and numerically. "Beginning in the fall of eighty-six," he said, "we shall offer a degree in Electrical Engineering. Within five years, I predict that we'll have an enrollment surpassing two thousand students."

International Campus

The investment into the Prescott Campus enabled Embry-Riddle to appeal to a greater segment of the nation. But if the University was going to reach students living outside the continental United States (particularly those serving at military bases), yet another approach had to be created.

Traditionally, Embry-Riddle attracted military personnel—especially those involved with some phase of aviation. It was natural, then, that the University find additional ways to serve this community. The International Campus provided one approach that worked.

Resident centers were established as early as 1970 at military bases throughout the United States and Europe. Without leaving the base, a member of the armed forces could attend classes, even complete all degree requirements for both the bachelor and masters degrees. The idea worked. Today, through the International Campus, Embry-Riddle

Taxiing at Love Field, Prescott, Arizona. Flight students at the Prescott campus train at Love Field, three miles away among the mountain scenery.

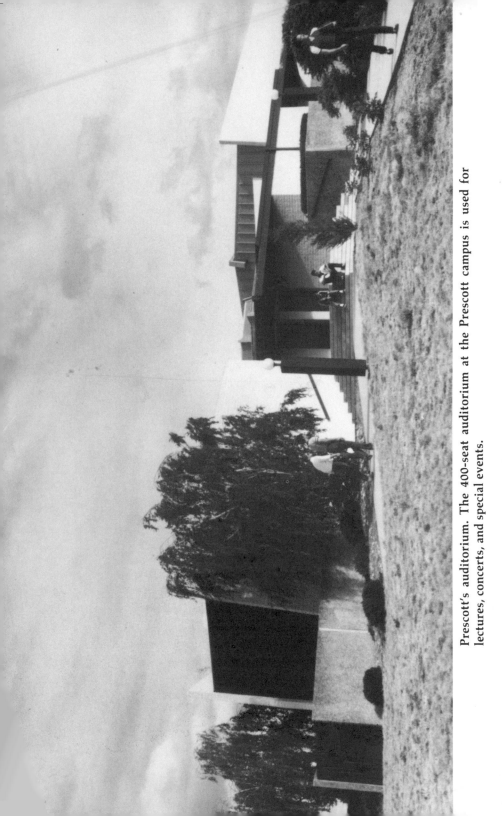

Prescott's auditorium. The 400-seat auditorium at the Prescott campus is used for lectures, concerts, and special events.

sponsors resident centers in over 80 locations, serving nearly 26,000 part-time students.

The International Campus reached out to another group of people who, because of careers and schedules, were unable to attend classes in a conventional campus environment. The Center for Independent Studies now allows nearly 1,000 men and women to study via self-teaching texts, individual counseling, and state-of-the-art computer-aided programs.

Chancellor Charles Williams of the International Campus sees this as the campus with the greatest potential for meeting the needs of aviation professionals today.

Due to increasing requests from graduates and other professionals in aviation, Embry-Riddle applied for, and received approval from SACS to offer a Master of Aviation Management degree during the summer of 1973. Arrangements were completed with Biscayne College in Miami to offer the first program.

Today, hundreds of students currently pursue graduate degrees in Aviation Management, Aeronautical Science, and Business Administration/Aviation.

Bunnell

Jack Hunt, who kept active his real estate license, was constantly on the lookout for property at a bargain price. One of those bargains was a lodge at a defunct amusement park in Bunnell, Florida, a rural community 20 miles north of the Daytona Beach Campus.

The "Marco Polo Lodge" at the intersection of Interstate 95 and the Old Dixie Highway was designed to house visitors to Marco Polo Park—a theme park located across the road. Unfortunately, no amusement center could compete with Walt Disney World in nearby Orlando. After operating for a bit more than one year, the executives of Marco Polo Park filed for bankruptcy. With the closing of the park, the lodge became virtually useless.

Mr. Jack White, one of the park's owners, approached President Hunt with an offer to sell it to the University for

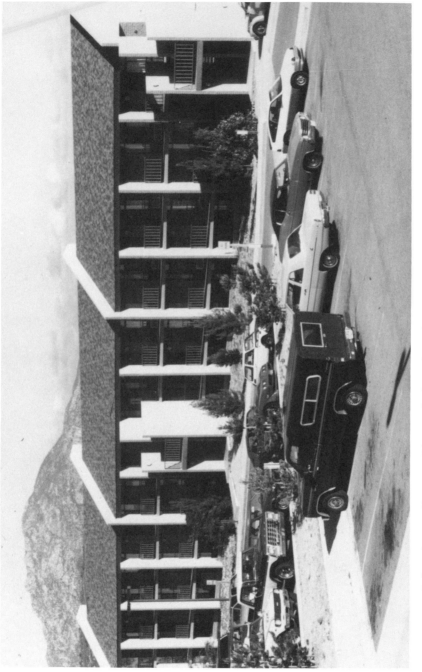

A dormitory at Prescott. The 454-bed residence hall on the Prescott campus was built in 1981.

the balance of the mortgage payments. In 1980 the agreement was signed.

The new Embry-Riddle "Main Campus" (as it was initially called) allowed certain departments to move from the overcrowded Daytona Beach Campus. The administrative offices and the International Campus were the first to relocate there. Others soon followed. By 1985, the "Executive Offices" (as it was renamed) housed the offices of the President and his staff, the International Campus, plus the departments that served all three campuses.

Growth in Daytona

Not only was Embry-Riddle offering programs in response to the needs of the times, but also the "mother campus" at Daytona Beach had to change in order to accommodate the increased enrollment that sometimes surpassed 5,000 students.

Classroom buildings, apartment complexes, a service park, full-service library, swimming pool, and parking facilities were among the more notable additions.

The flight line includes 35 Cessna 172s, five twin-engine Piper Seminoles, and three cabin-class twin-engine Cessna 303 Crusaders. In addition, both single engine and multi-engine simulators allow students to gain valuable instrument time at a fraction of the cost of the "in-flight" alternative.

Simulators were only part of the advanced technology employed at the school. Students could earn an associate's and bachelor's degrees in Avionics.

Three separate rooms house the digital, micro-processing, and communications laboratory, plus the linear-components and semi-conductor laboratory, and the avionics laboratory.

Although most of the growth was in the form of new buildings and more complex aircraft, the University insisted that each student be required to study English, history, philosophy, literature, psychology, sociology, and other similar disciplines. President Hunt insisted that aviation education should train the whole person. It was a principle not unlike that of J. Paul Riddle who, a half-century earlier, learned to appreciate the importance of all phases of aviation.

Jack Hunt maintained that nobody can really teach; all he or she could hope to do was motivate students to learn. "One of the most powerful motivational appeals is aviation," he said.

A pragmatic proof that his philosophy was sound was the incorporation of the "Upward Bound" program on the Daytona Beach Campus. Beginning in 1975, area high school students, who lacked the motivation to study, assembled on the Campus on Saturday mornings and each weekday for six weeks in the summer. Here they were taught the basic skills of reading, writing, and math, using aviation as a practical application. When the students took regular flights in one of the University aircraft, they could see for themselves, for instance, why knowledge in geometry was necessary if you want to plot a course, and why reading for understanding is a "must" if you want to learn the limits of the aircraft before you leave the security of the ground.

The number of applications to the program have increased each year, partly due to the national acclaim it has received in the media. Over 90 percent of its graduates are accepted into the colleges and universities of their choice. Before "Upward Bound," each student was a prime candidate to join the ranks of high school dropouts.

One of the more remarkable changes on the Daytona Beach Campus was a decree from the Federal Aviation Administration in 1979 that granted self-examining authority for private, commercial, instrument, and multi-engine certificates. In 1983, the self-examining authority extended to license instructors in these areas. This unique exception means that a student with high aptitude can save thousands of dollars in the search for advanced certificates.

This one pronouncement by the F.A.A. demonstrated more than anything else that Embry-Riddle had matured to a

Pictured here is the Riddle Ramp at the Daytona Beach campus in 1986. Visible are twin-engine Cessna 303 Crusaders and Cessna 172 Skyhawks. The Tine Davis Building is in the background.

level that must have surpassed even the wildest dreams of its leaders.

A new era

On the morning of January 7, 1984, four ROTC cadets solemnly marched to the main flagpole on the Daytona Beach Campus. They raised the colors to the top, then slowly lowered them to half-mast. President Jack Hunt, age 65, died at his home following a year-long battle with cancer.

Many of the thousands who gathered for memorial services at the Daytona Beach and Prescott Campuses openly wept.

Jack Hunt was many things to many people. But one thing was certain. His life was the University, particularly the students.

"He often shunned his title when introducing himself," said his widow, Lynne. "He simply stated he was involved with the administration of the University. 'Titles scare people,' he would say. 'It's easier to find out what's on a student's mind over a game of handball than by calling him into the President's office.'"

Jack Hunt's appreciation for the student became most apparent when he recommended to the Board of Trustees that students be represented as full voting members of the Board. The recommendation was approved and put into practice long before most other academic institutions ever considered such a step.

In keeping with the theme begun by J. Paul Riddle in the 1920s, Hunt remained alert to the potential contribution of women to aviation and higher education. One of the employees, Dianne Thompson, began as a clerk/typist at the University in 1971. Later, she applied for the position as Secretary to the President and was given the job.

"President Hunt recognized something in me I didn't know was there," she said. "He gave me an opportunity to grow and to develop a confidence I didn't know I had."

In 1976, with the urging of Hunt, Mrs. Thompson was

General Kenneth Tallman was named president of Embry-Riddle in 1985.

elected Corporate Secretary of Embry-Riddle, making her an officer of the University.

The President remained alert to other values as well. Two months before he died, Jack Hunt was honored by the Daytona Beach community when the Regional Airport Terminal was named in his honor.

At the ceremony of dedication, a tired, thin, gravel-voiced Jack Hunt was still able to echo his vision of the University: "Embry-Riddle doesn't belong to me or to the Board of Trustees," he said. "It belongs to everybody in the United States. And that, ladies and gentlemen, is a big responsibility."

Shortly before January 7, when he knew the end was near, Jack Hunt requested that in lieu of purchasing flowers, donors give their contributions in his memory to the construction of the new library on the Daytona Beach Campus and to scholarships for deserving students. "Concern for the students was foremost in his mind—even in the face of death," said John Fidel, a Vice President for the University.

Tributes to President Hunt poured in from throughout the United States when the A.P. wires announced the news of his death. Aviators, educators, politicians, public figures, and perhaps most important, students, praised his accomplishments.

Dr. Jeffrey H. Ledewitz, who took the reins as Interim President, spoke for the entire Embry-Riddle family when he addressed the next meeting of the Board of Trustees:

> A university is a living thing. Fragile in infancy, it grows in strength as it matures. When guided with wisdom and vision in the formative years, it can develop a character and sense of purpose that will enable it to meet successfully the challenges of a changing world. Embry-Riddle Aeronautical University was indeed fortunate to have such a leader in President Jack Hunt.

In January, 1985, the Board elected Lieutenant General Kenneth L. Tallman as next President.

7

Lift-Off to the Future

J. Paul Riddle today. The co-founder of Embry-Riddle as he nears his eighty-fifth birthday.

"The biggest challenge is getting the program in high gear by motivating everybody to work as a team. I'm confident we can do it."

—Kenneth L. Tallman, 1986

The story of Embry-Riddle Aeronautical University is the result of a rare combination of dedicated pioneers, each of whom left a unique mark. People such as J. Paul Riddle, T. Higbee Embry, John McKay, Isabel McKay, and Jack Hunt were determined, individualistic, oft times stubborn people who proved to be the right leaders for their times. In fact, it is hard for us to conceive of the University as we know it without them.

In keeping with this tradition, the Board of Trustees, at its meeting in January 1985, selected as the new President of the University, Lt. Gen. Kenneth L. Tallman.

Tallman, a native of Omaha, earned a solid reputation in the armed services, rising to the rank of Lieutenant General. As a graduate with a bachelor's degree from the United States Military Academy and a masters from George Washington University, as an Air Force fighter pilot, Commander, and Personnel Manager, he brought with him a firsthand appreciation for the military, aviation, and academics.

Aviation school administration was nothing new to General Tallman. Prior to his appointment at Embry-Riddle, he distinguished himself as Superintendent of the United States Air Force Academy and as President of the Spartan School of Aeronautics.

General Tallman brings to the University a charismatic leadership that elicits enthusiastic cooperation from staff, faculty, and students alike. He shuns any hint of a dictatorial, "Do it my way or else" posture, and opts, instead, for listening to the advice of his staff. Although he sits at the top of the administrative totem pole, he is not above going out of his way to help students, employees or family members with personal problems.

General Tallman's style might be unlike that of some others who don the cap and gown of a university president or even his predecessors in many ways, yet he shares that one philosophy that has guided the School ever since Mr. Riddle first climbed into the back seat of a Waco-9; namely, that aviation is more than just flying airplanes. Biplanes have vanished from the flight line, and mechanics who once tuned engines by ear now calibrate by computer. Yet Gen. Tallman is dedicated to the proposition that Embry-Riddle's basic approach to aviation education will not change.

Like the others who went before him, he carries an appreciation for the entire scope of aviation, including air science, maintenance, engineering, management, computer science, avionics, meterology, and, of course, safety.

But General Tallman has added a new emphasis as a response to the demands of the times. "Although Embry-Riddle intends to remain focused on aviation," he says, "it also plans to expand its curriculum to include aerospace." Tallman explained that aerospace is a future of aviation that many institutions have overlooked. "If we are going to make any sort of impact in the twenty-first century," he says, "we must lead the way in education for the age of aerospace. It's past the time that we think of aerospace as something apart from aviation."

Lift-Off to the Future

Eric Doten, Chancellor of the Daytona Beach Campus, picks up on this theme: "Next fall we will be introducing an Engineering Physics degree program as an initial step into the aerospace arena. Additionally, we will consider developing courses in such areas as aerospace maintenance and space law. While some may regard the current emphasis on space travel as merely a public relations effort of the Government, we see this as an opportunity for future development in areas that we haven't yet imagined."

"It is also important that we not forget the value of research," adds Tallman." Even though we are primarily a teaching institution, we should expand our efforts in research in order to be more responsive to the aerospace industry, attract grant monies and equipment, and provide development opportunities for our faculty." As a preliminary to expanded research activities, Embry-Riddle plans to introduce a Master of Science degree in Aeronautical Engineering commencing in the fall of 1986. Other opportunities for applied research will be explored in the human factors engineering area.

Embry-Riddle also plans to seek growth and expansion through its International Campus which services adult education needs. President Tallman points out that "this is a fast-growing market, with more and more people seeking opportunities to complete requirements for bachelor and masters degrees in aviation-oriented programs. As an adjunct to this initiative, Tallman intends to place greater emphasis and resources into professional programs for the aviation-minded adult through workshops, seminars and short courses. "In this way," he explains, "we will maintain curriculum relevance, faculty currency, and aviation industry rapport."

In March 1986, Embry-Riddle was paid what might be considered its highest stamp of approval by the Federal Aviation Administration when it was awarded the management training and support services contract for the FAA. The center will be constructed in Palm Coast, Florida, located approximately 30 miles north of the Daytona Beach Campus.

"This contract is for thirty-five million dollars," reported Dr. L. William Motzel, Vice President for Special Projects, who was responsible for writing the proposal.

In addition, that same month, the University received a letter from FAA Administrator Donald D. Engen announcing the award of a $500,000 grant to begin development of an airway science simulation laboratory. "This will give the University a unique resource for helping students to understand the comprehensive dimensions of the national airspace system and will allow them to develop judgment and team skills in that environment," said Dr. Motzel, who also wrote the proposal for this project.

"These two initiatives in support of FAA requirements will provide many opportunities for greater interface with the aviation/aerospace industry, both nationally and internationally," says Gen. Tallman. "I visualize they will help us continue to lead the way in aviation education as our air transportation system expands into the next century."

"The whole process of growth for Embry-Riddle is a multi-faceted operation," says President Tallman, "and the biggest challenge is getting the program in high gear by motivating everybody to work as a team. I'm confident we can do it."

As zealous as these dreams might appear to the outsider, those who know and love aviation, especially aviation education, realize that looking back at Embry-Riddle 60 years from now, one could possibly say: "We did this . . . and more."

And why not? After all, for others, the sky's the limit; for Embry-Riddle, it's home.

Index

Index

Index